Practical Life for Parents

A Pocket Guide for Parenting
Real-Life Moments

BRIDIE GAUTHIER

For the A-Team – Kristin, Eric, Cecelia, and Sharahn
Who allow me to do what we do every day
And for Kai, who reminds me why we do it

CONTENTS

ACKNOWLEDGMENTS

I would like to thank everyone who has supported me in writing this book. Thank you to Eric, for encouraging me to take on the project in the first place. Thank you to Kristin, for fifteen years of insight, inspiration, and most of all, friendship. Thank you to Sharahn for always seeing and pointing out the things that I do not notice about myself, and for trusting me to educate your children. Thank you to Cecelia for being a great coach, cohort, and always a firm shoulder when I need one. Thank you to Cindy and Lex, for being my cheerleaders at exactly the right moment. Thank you to Sammy, for listening to me talk about this book non-stop on our trips to and from Manhattan and for asking questions that made me think. Thank you to Kai and Sidra, for giving me the chance to put these words into real-life practice. Thank you to Mum and Dad, for well, everything. Thank you to my best friend Domenic for forty years of unconditional friendship. Thank you to Charlie for your very kind and thoughtful endorsement, and to Mary Alice and all the kids and teachers of the Batey, for allowing me to bring these ideas to your tiny corner of the world. Thank you to Theresa, Katie, Marva, Maia, Evelyna and Ilya, for your brilliant editing and artistic talents. Thank you to my husband Joe, for 20 years of always letting me be me, and for tolerating with love and patience (almost) every time I have told him he is parenting "wrong." Finally, thank you to all the parents and children I have had the privilege of knowing and teaching over the past three decades.

I adore you all, and could not have done this without you.

)

INTRODUCTION

In my 30 years as an educator, I have heard one question from moms and dads more than any other: "What should I do when…?"

As a parent in this day and age, you have a wealth of parenting guides, books on educational philosophy, and online resources at your disposal. What you do not have is the time to sit down and actually read them. While it would be wonderful to be able to carefully digest the pages of a psychology textbook detailing the stages of cognitive development of your preschooler, when said preschooler is tired, hungry, late for soccer practice, and you still have not finished that presentation due for your 8 a.m. board meeting, the psychology textbook collects another day's worth of dust.

Practical Life for Parents, is written as a quick reference guide to concisely sum up what is happening in many of the most common parenting situations, and cut to the chase of what you can actually <u>do</u> in the moment.

If children came with a user manual, parenting would be easy and my book would be unnecessary. They do not. So, for anyone navigating the waters of parenting a young child, I hope that *Practical Life for Parents,* can offer you a little peace of mind as well as some useful strategies to help you out along the way.

THE SEVEN SECOND RULE
-PROCESSING INFORMATION-

Standing in line at the coffee shop recently, I overheard a dad asking his daughter if she wanted a doughnut. He then immediately asked her what kind she wanted and then, barely letting enough time pass to take a breath, began listing the different flavor choices. Whether riding the subway, walking down the street, or like my experience at the coffee shop, there are many instances to observe a grownup asking a child a question. In more than a few of those instances, the adult then immediately asks another question, or even answers the original question for their child.

What do I need to know? Young children require at least seven seconds to take in what has been said, process that information, and then formulate a response. As adults we tend to forget this and often follow one question with another, then another, and another, or simply answer the question before the little one has had the chance to do so. How many times a day can you catch yourself saying something like: "Are you hungry?"; "Do you want a snack?"; "Do you want some raisins?"; "You want some raisins, right?"

What can I do? In this example, you will have much more success by simply asking your child, "Are you hungry?" and then pausing to give her ample opportunity to process and answer the question. More often than not, you will discover something new about your child, understand more about how she thinks, or even learn something new yourself from an answer that you were not expecting. So pause for your own seven-second delay and remember that getting your child's answer is far more important than getting the right answer.

WHEN "OK" IS NOT OKAY
-GIVING CLEAR DIRECTION-

The phrase "my child refuses to do anything I ask" is not unique to you. It happens to the best of us. Certain changes in behavior are innate and have to be expected (and tolerated) as young children go through different milestones of development; however, there are definitely some simple strategies that you can implement to make life a little easier for you both. Try counting how many times in a day that you use "okay" to end a directive to your child. How often do you say: "Let's brush your teeth, okay?"; "Put your toys away, okay?"; "Let's get ready for bed, okay?" Ever wonder why you get resistance?

What do I need to know? As adults we all say and do these kinds of things without giving them a second thought; however, to a child, whose level of understanding is still completely literal, it makes a world of difference. By simply adding "okay" to a statement, you have unintentionally turned what you have just said into a question, thereby making it a choice. As with any choice, you have now just given him permission to say "No!"

What can I do? Eliminate "okay" from verbal instruction to your child when your expectation is that he actually must comply with your directive. This removes the possibility of it being perceived as a choice. "It's time to brush your teeth" is a much clearer and stronger statement. It tells your child exactly what is expected, when it is expected, and offers no other alternative. In other words, use fewer words and when you say "okay" make sure that you mean it.

YOU CAN NEVER WATCH TV AGAIN!
- UNREALISTIC CONSEQUENCES-

Regardless of how effective you are in setting firm limits, there will still be moments when your child acts out. Children experiment with their developing autonomy and growing sense of independence by testing the limits that you set. When it inevitably happens, what matters most is that you respond with a realistic consequence, and then follow through on it.

What do I need to know? One of the biggest mistakes that any adult can make is to threaten a consequence to unacceptable behavior that cannot be rendered. Failing to follow through on a consequence with a young child is tantamount to handing away all your power as a parent. As soon as one consequence slips past undelivered, your word no longer has meaning. When Allie just will not stop chasing the cat up the Christmas tree because to her it is absolutely hilarious, and the tree inevitably comes crashing to the ground, screaming at the top of your lungs that you are cancelling Christmas is probably not a realistic consequence unless you are actually prepared to toss out the tree, return the presents, and order a pizza on December 25th.

What can I do? Be clear with your child about exactly what is and is not acceptable behavior. Do not waiver on the boundaries you have set no matter how difficult it may seem, and never, never, never, threaten a consequence that you cannot, or will not, deliver. Cancelling Christmas is completely unrealistic. A much more effective consequence is to inform Allie that she will now use her allowance to replace the broken ornaments, then march her straight to the nearest department store with piggy bank in hand. This kind of reality-based consequence will not only give your word power, it will also make a concrete impression in Allie's mind that will have a much more lasting impact on her future decisions.

THIS OR THAT
-AUTHENTIC CHOICES-

Elegantly said by Dr. Sandra Crosser, "in the lives of young children there are many you may nots." You may not stay home alone. You may not have chocolate chip cookies for dinner. You may not cross the street by yourself. Because there are so many things a two or three-year-old may not be permitted to do simply for reasons of health or safety, it can be difficult for little ones to feel in control of their lives. However, this is exactly the time that a child needs to develop a sense of being a competent, independent, individual.

What do I need to know? One of the best ways to develop this necessary independence is to make choices. It is important for young children to make choices so that they will begin to feel some sense of control, which contributes to healthy personality development by building a sense of autonomy. Providing choices will naturally reduce a child's need to try to gain control in negative ways; however, those choices must be authentic. So what is an authentic choice? An authentic choice is simply that – it's real. It is a choice a child makes that actually matters and is honored.

What can I do? Pay attention to the number of times you offer your child a false choice. False choices are really no choice at all, yet they happen all the time. They happen when you ask, "Are you ready for bed?", or "Do you want to brush your teeth?", when in fact not going to bed and not brushing teeth are *not* an option. When offering your child a choice, it is crucial to offer an authentic choice and respect his decision. Just like we discussed when ending sentences with "okay", never ask, "Do you want to…" unless you are prepared for "No!" as an answer. Instead, create opportunities for success. When you offer your child two or three real suggestions, then his choice can be respected. Going to bed cannot be a choice; however, offering two different pair of pajamas to choose from, certainly can be. It is equally important to make clear to children when there is no choice. For example, when safety or health is at risk, or when it is simply time to follow a rule or routine. Playing with matches is *not* a choice and no matter how apocalyptic the tantrum, a three-year-old is not in charge of that decision.

Defining clear and firm limits, coupled with offering authentic choices helps young children to develop self-confidence, the skills for independent thinking, and a sense of accountability.

Hint: When offering a choice to a very young child, and there is one option that you as the parent favor, offer that option *last*. Toddlers and preschoolers will almost always choose the last thing you say.

"I'M SORRY" AND OTHER USELESS STATEMENTS
-TEACHING ACCOUNTABILITY-

Think about the number of times you overhear an adult telling a child to "Say you're sorry!" Teaching accountability for one's actions is extremely important so that your child can grow up to become a compassionate, empathetic, and successful member of society. However, accountability must be taught effectively and in a way that makes sense in the mind of your little one.

What do I need to know? Young children live in a literal and concrete world. Saying "sorry" does not truly resonate because toddlers and preschoolers are not yet capable of understanding abstract reasoning. They quickly learn to parrot the words "I'm sorry;" however, at an early age all that it really means in their little minds is that those are the words you are supposed to say "when you are bad".

What can I do? Take the abstractness out of being accountable by offering your child concrete ways to atone for a wrong-doing. If your son squabbles with a playmate, rather than simply apologizing, have him get a tissue for his friend. He might not fully understand "I'm sorry;" however, he can certainly see that the tissue fixes his friend's tears. When your daughter injures her little brother while arguing over a toy, allow her to participate in the first-aid by opening the Band-Aid for him, or helping him to hold the ice pack. Measures such as these will give your child a concrete and understandable way to be accountable, and to learn empathy and compassion at an age-appropriate level.

"LOOK AT ME MOM!"
-ESTABLISHING RELATEDNESS-

It is tough to be two or three years old. You cannot reach the faucet on the sink, you cannot get things out of the refrigerator on your own, and seemingly everyone is bigger than you are. Little ones are navigating this great big world for the first time and everything to them is a challenge.

What do I need to know? Operating in a world designed for grownups can be overwhelming for a young child. How difficult would it be to do your job if everything in the office was just slightly out of reach, and every time your boss needed to speak with you he towered over you and loudly barked directives down at you? Your experience of life at work would be pretty difficult and definitely stressful.

What can I do? There are many ways to make the physical environment in your home less daunting for your child: place toys on a low, reachable shelf; put child-sized bottles of milk or water on the bottom shelf of the refrigerator. There are also many things you can personally do as a parent to reduce the overwhelm and establish relatedness. One of the most crucial actions is to make meaningful eye contact. When speaking to your child, actually get down to his level by crouching, kneeling, or bending and look him right in the eyes. Speak in a clear, gentle tone that lets him know you are speaking to him and only him, and that this conversation is valuable and important to you. Making this one small change to the way you interact with your child will have tremendous impact on the quality of your conversations, and in turn will trickle through all other aspects of your relationship.

"HOW WAS YOUR DAY?"
-THE ART OF CONVERSATION-

When greeting a child at pick-up time from school or an activity, it may seem quite natural to ask an open-ended question such as, "How was your day?" To an adult it seems quite logical to ask the ones you love about their day when you come back together; however, for a young child these kinds of open-ended questions can be very confusing.

What do I need to know? A child who is younger than five years old, lives in the moment. This means that when you come to pick her up from school or a play date, she is enjoying the moment of seeing you again. If, in that moment, you ask an open-ended question such as, "How was your day?", your little one can be easily caught off-guard and unable to answer your question. In a young child's mind, she is enjoying the present and not recapping the events of the day (Moudry, 2015). The ability to recap past events is a milestone in the development of a much older child. If an answer cannot be formulated in that very moment, often children can feel stressed and may come up with an activity that they remember from the past, or a staple answer that has worked before such as "I had snack."

What can I do? Model the behavior you are seeking. Greet your child with a hug and say, "Hello, it's nice to see you." She may respond with something similar. On your way home, wait patiently, offering your child time to open up if she chooses. If your child remains quiet, continue modeling by offering a description of your day. "I was working in my office today" or "I enjoyed having lunch with my colleague." Then pause and wait. She may then ask you a question, or may follow your lead and share something similar. The important piece is to refrain from asking questions. Making statements will help your child understand what might be notable. Over time, she will start to offer tidbits, begin to understand the art of conversation, and a pattern of exchange will emerge. Patiently allowing young children to develop their own ideas in their own time will teach appropriate social discourse and lead to conversations that prove much more meaningful for both of you.

A HIGHLY SENSITIVE RECORDING DEVICE
-COMPREHENSION PRECEDES EXPRESSION-

One of the easiest things for adults to forget is to monitor the subject matter of conversations that take place within earshot of children. I do not only mean inappropriate or adult subjects like death, illness, sex, and gossip. I also mean matters of common courtesy. Think about how often adults speak about a child right in front of him. Such conduct would never be acceptable if the person being spoken about was another adult, so why do it to a child?

What do I need to know? Your little one has ears. Just because your child is not speaking yet, it is absolutely not an indicator of what he is able to understand. Comprehension far exceeds expression. In fact, recent research indicates that infants as young as six months old can fully understand the meaning of a wide variety of words (Gavaghan, 2012).

What can I do? Remember the golden rule and do unto your child as you would have your family, friends, or coworkers do unto you. Do speak *to* your child; however, never speak *about* your child if he is present. Showing your little one this kind of courtesy is not only socially appropriate, kind, and respectful of his feelings, but also teaches your child to respond to you in the same way.

As early on as possible, make it a habit to never do or say anything in the presence of your child that you would not want him to then turn around and either do or repeat himself. Your child is part of your family and during the course of any day, he will certainly overhear conversations that you are having with others. Keep in mind that even the youngest children will take in your every word and action, and once these little ones master expressive language, they will also repeat everything that you say or do. If you do not believe this fact, just ask any preschool teacher to share some of the stories her students repeat from home!

From a real-life, five-year-old to his classmate: *"Let's play house. You be the mommy and I'll be the neighbor who comes over to visit in the night."*

"I'M BORED!"
-DON'T BE DUPED BY FALSE STATEMENTS -

When your child makes a declaration such as, "I'm bored!" or "it's boring!", it can be quite alarming. As a parent, you naturally only want what is best for your child's education, cognitive development, and creative and social growth; however, be wary of overreacting to these kinds of false and attention-grabbing claims.

What do I need to know? Your child will learn very early in life exactly how to push your buttons, and will do it as often as possible if you give the desired reaction. Statements such as the classic "I'm bored" are one of the easiest ways for young children to gain attention and evoke a reaction from parents. Children quickly learn to parrot these words, but they do not understand them. Young children are simply not at a level of cognitive development to actually comprehend what it means to be "bored."

What can I do? Ask. When your little one loudly announces that she does not want to go to playgroup because "it's boring", rather than overreacting and immediately pulling her out of the class, or scheduling a conference to discuss ideas for possible curriculum improvement with the teacher, simply ask the question, "What does that mean?" The safe bet is that she will not be able to give you an answer.

At some point your child will certainly reach the appropriate level of development to actually explain to you what it means to be "bored." Then will be the time to listen to and honor what she is saying. Until that time, when your child makes an alarming statement, asking for further explanation will often give you greater insight into what is really going on. You will likely discover the source is something much more fundamental such as she overheard you saying you are going shopping while she is at playgroup and she really just wants to go with you.

"LET YOUR FRIEND HAVE A TURN!"
-THE REALITIES OF SHARING-

Sharing is a very important topic for parents because it is often presumed to be an indicator of a child's successful social and emotional development. Parents often worry that if their children do not share well or take turns, then they will not have any friends. Naturally, no parent ever wants to see that happen.

What do I need to know? Sharing and taking turns are important skills; however, adults often expect them of children far earlier than is age appropriate. Many parents will insist that their children share their belongings with other children. What does this really teach them? From Montessori Unlimited – when you insist that your child share, you are taking away from him an opportunity to give from the heart. When you restrain yourself and trust the children, you may notice that they often resolve the issue on their own. Keep in mind:

- Two and three-year-olds begin experimenting with various sharing techniques, such as taking turns and trading toys for short periods of time.

- Three and four-year-olds begin to cooperate. They understand that giving does not mean giving up, and are more willing to give and take with friends.

- Four and five-year-olds grasp the concept of sharing very well. They play cooperatively with their friends and are willing to share their possessions.

What can I do? Encourage sharing but definitely do not force it. How would you feel if someone handed you the keys to drive a brand new Ferrari and then five minutes later told you that you have to give it to your friend and if you refuse, you are being naughty and selfish? Little children are experiencing the world for the first time and everything to them is as new and exciting as your brand new Ferrari. A reluctant sharer may just be really excited to play with his cool new toy, and forcing him to turn around and immediately give it away before he is finished enjoying it can send the message that his needs are not as important as his friend's needs.

Keep in mind that forcing a child to comply is *not* the same as teaching generosity. Talk with your little one and acknowledge that sometimes it is hard to share. Use empathy rather than scolding to encourage sharing. It is equally important that you provide your child with opportunities to <u>not</u> share. Put away a few special toys before a play date begins so they are simply not available options. Most importantly, incorporate role-modeling and share with your child. Generosity is taught by example, so exercise the behavior you wish your child to exhibit by sharing food, storybooks, or an extra special "something" that is reserved only for the two of you.

SHORT GOODBYES AND LONG HELLOS
-DEALING WITH SEPARATION-

Separating from a parent or caregiver can be a trying experience for a child and seeing your little one upset can be heartbreaking for you as a parent. It is completely normal when you see or hear your child crying, to want to burst through the door of her playgroup with hugs and apologies, and head directly to the nearest ice cream shop to atone for your terrible sin of having left in the first place. Fudge ripple is not the answer.

What do I need to know? As adults we naturally forget what it is like to think like a child. Young children cannot extrapolate and transfer information from one setting to another. Their little brains are just not wired that way yet. Just because your daughter understands that mommy or daddy always comes home, it does not mean that she can automatically transfer that knowledge to understand that you will always come back to her new gymnastics class. She has to learn that information all over again in this brand new setting.

What can I do? When beginning a new class or activity, remember that your child needs to see you leave and come back, and the next day leave and come back, and the next day leave and come back, until the trust in your eventual return is established. It will take time and patience. Children who have the greatest difficulty with separation are most often those whose parent's leave-taking is prolonged and indecisive.

Remember: "short good-byes and long hellos." Be clear by making your departure positive and brief. Have a goodbye routine to help your little one to feel more in control of the situation. On the way to the class, explain exactly what is going to happen: "Today is Monday. You are going to school with your friends and then I will pick you up to go to the park." Say goodbye with a brief, reassuring hug, a kiss, and a big smile, and depart with intent. Save extended hugs and kisses as a special treat for you both at pick-up time. Finally, be sure that you are on time for pick-up. Anxiety can build up again at the end of the day and being punctual will help your little one to feel safe.

WHEN CONSISTENCY IS INCONSISTENT
-DEALING WITH DISRUPTION TO ROUTINE-

Routine is very important for young children. Meal schedules, sleep schedules, and being on time for school, all work to give young children a sense of security by establishing consistency and reliability in their day. As hard as you work to establish a consistent routine for your child, life often gets in the way. Holidays arrive, company comes to visit, and vacations happen.

What do I need to know? The influx of gifts, guests, travel, or celebrations, although thoroughly enjoyable, can also be overwhelming for young children. No matter how good your intentions, grandmas will spoil, bedtimes will slide, and too many goodies will be eaten. Stressing over these inevitabilities is pointless.

What can I do? During a disruptive times, maintain one routine. Whether it is bedtime, nap time, story time, or bath time, choose one of your family's usual routines and stick with it. Evening bedtime is often the hardest to keep in place when there are relatives visiting or parties to attend, so choose one that will be easier to maintain. Then, as holiday season or your trip to Disney winds to a close, gradually begin to work the rest of your child's routines back into his daily schedule.

LET DOWN-TIME BE DOWN
-KEEPING HOME, HOME AND SCHOOL, SCHOOL-

Many parents feel pressure or concern to replicate an academic environment like a classroom setting in the home. Trying to recreate the school experience at home is never successful. Keep home, home and school, school.

What do I need to know? When your preschooler comes home from a full day of learning and fun with her classmates and teachers, the last thing she needs or wants is a 20-minute drill with alphabet flash cards, or a pop-quiz on the Periodic Table.

What can I do? Play with your child. Take the opportunity of being home together to actually enjoy doing a little bit of nothing. Put the electronics away and enjoy one another. Read a favorite book, do a simple craft or cooking project, or simply roll around on the bed and cuddle. These moments are every bit as important for your child's social and emotional development as her daily math, science, or language lessons in the classroom. Researcher Sergio Pellis of University of Lethbridge, concludes that unstructured play is necessary for brain development. Play changes the connections of the neurons in the prefrontal cortex and without the play experience, those neurons are not changed. These neurological changes during childhood help wire the brain's executive control center, which has a critical role in regulating emotions, making plans, and solving problems. So, play helps to prepare a young child's brain for life, love, and even schoolwork (Hamilton, 2014).

If your concern is maintaining some consistency between what happens at home and what happens at school, simply ask. Regardless of which educational style you have chosen for your child, your teachers are wonderful resources. Any talented teacher, from any pedagogical background, can certainly offer you simple ideas to help you maintain a consistent philosophical approach between home and school, without you having to run out and purchase a full complement of classroom supplies and activities.

"WHERE DO BABIES COME FROM?"
-ANSWERING DIFFICULT QUESTIONS-

At some point your little one is going to start asking difficult questions, usually, at the most inopportune time and place. As children begin to develop the cognitive skills necessary to reason, two of the most common subjects that they become curious about are birth and death.

Birth – As children move from the egocentric stage of toddlerhood to curious preschooler, they naturally start to wonder about many topics, including birth. They notice babies, pregnant mommies, or maybe even have a new sibling, and they start to ask questions.

What do I need to know? What you want your child to know about conception and birth is a very personal choice. No matter where you land in your belief about the information your child should have on the subject, remember with young children less is more. You can always add, but you can never subtract.

What can I do? When your child catches you off guard by loudly asking "Mommy, where do babies come from?" in the middle of your sister's wedding, step one is to stop and breathe. The best advice I ever received on answering this question came from one of the most brilliant women I know (thank you Kristin). The answer: "From the hospital." This will in no way end your inevitable discussion of the topic, but it will certainly buy you enough time to get to a more appropriate location, think about what you do and do not want him to know at this stage, and to prepare your answer.

Death – Another very difficult topic for parents is addressing death. Moms and dads find themselves not only dealing with their own grief, but also confronted with having to explain it to a young child.

What do I need to know? How to appropriately deal with this subject is much more clear-cut than that of birth. Your answer should be based in what the reality is for your child at that precise moment, and should depend directly on your child's actual capabilities for understanding.

What can I do? Very young children have no idea what death is and explaining it to them at this stage is not appropriate. A two-year-old is not capable of understanding that grandma passed away and the best, first answer that you can give when she asks where grandma is, is to simply say, "Grandma isn't here." Naturally your personal beliefs will eventually factor into discussion of the subject with your child; however, the key is to start with minimal information.

Older children eventually start to understand the subject of death. They get that grandma is not coming back. They may even understand more, depending upon how much conversation about grandma's passing they witness, whether grandma was ill for an extended period of time, and whether or not they attend the funeral.

Regardless of what you decide is appropriate for your family, be prepared that an older child will likely start asking other questions such as, "Am I going to die?" or "Are you going to die, daddy?" Here, remove your personal beliefs from the equation and answer with a firm "No." If a simple no does not satisfy, then continue the conversation by explaining that dying happens to people who are very, very old or very, very sick. Worrying about dying or losing a parent is an extremely traumatic, completely unfair, and absolutely unnecessary burden for your four-year-old. Children will eventually grow to understand the reality of life. There is no need to rush it.

It is important to note that many young children will *say* things that lead grownups to believe they are able to understand very complicated subjects. They do not. Young children may repeat things that they see or overhear; however, this is absolutely *not* an indicator of comprehension. Lead with the most basic, concrete information possible. When it comes to sharing information about difficult subjects like birth or death, remember: you can always do it, but you can never undo it.

"NO." IS A COMPLETE SENTENCE
-THE IMPORTANCE OF BOUNDARIES-

Many parents find it very hard to say "No." and most admit it is attributed to the behavior that will likely follow the "No." When your child has a meltdown, especially in public, it is easy to fall into the habit of just giving in to make it stop. Some parents also fall into the habit of over rationalizing, or over negotiating, feeling that their child deserves an explanation, or believing that somehow an explanation will make a light bulb go off in his head and the problem will be solved. Other parents fall into the trap of wanting to be their child's friend. Children do not need mom or dad to be their friend. What they need is for you to teach them how to appropriately act and react, so that they can successfully make and keep friends of their own.

What do I need to know? There is absolutely nothing wrong with saying "No." Children need boundaries from adults to feel safe and secure. These limits are essential for children to learn how to function socially. It is our job as parents and educators to determine what those boundaries will be at home and in the classroom and within this relationship, it is your child's role to push the set boundaries. By pushing boundaries, children learn to compromise, negotiate, and accept authority (Rachelle, 2015). Boundaries set children up with realistic social awareness. "No." is part of life. Children are going to hear it at school, within friendships, relationships, eventually at work, and it is critical that they hear it from their parents first. When you say "No." to your child, the message he receives is: "I am the adult. I know what is best for you and because I love you, I am saying No."

What can I do? First and foremost remain calm and stand firmly by your "No." Becoming upset or yelling at your child only negates your authority. Do not negotiate with a child who is upset. Speak gently yet firmly and encourage your child to express what he finds upsetting. Once the tears have quelled, then negotiation can begin, if appropriate to the situation. If you had to say "No." to a chocolate chip cookie for breakfast, then negotiating a more appropriate time to have said cookie is reasonable. However, if you have said "No." to sticking a paperclip in the light socket, obviously that "No." has to stand.

Saying "No." to your child can be very challenging and very frustrating. It is extremely important not to take the resulting tears or lashing-out personally. One of the saddest blog posts I have ever read was written by a mom who crawled into bed with her little boy each night to whisper apologies and promise "to be a better mommy tomorrow" because she just did not know how to refrain from losing her temper. Avoid making accusatory statements like, "You are so naughty"; or speaking in absolutes like, "You never listen", or "You always misbehave." Keep in mind that your role as a parent is to teach your child how to act and react. Speak to your child in the same manner that you wish your boss would speak to you and despite the reaction, do not feel pressure to over-talk. Silence is often your best course of action and can make your point far better than too many words. Keep in mind that "No." truly is a complete sentence.

WE ALL SCREAM FOR ICE CREAM
-MODELING EXPECTED BEHAVIOR-

At some point we have all witnessed an adult respond to a screaming, crying, child by screaming back in frustration. Maybe we have even done it ourselves. Tantrums, especially public ones, can be aggravating and embarrassing for you as a parent and it is completely natural to become upset; however, your reaction to the situation will dictate how the rest of it unfolds.

What do I need to know? Children will model your behavior. They learn by observing and internalizing information from their surroundings, especially from the grownups in their lives. This fact remains true even in the midst of the most cataclysmic tantrum.

What can I do? When your child commences to wail, lower your voice to almost a whisper. Even when you want to pull your own hair out or cry yourself, maintain a calm demeanor and speak to her in a soft, soothing tone. By no means can every situation be immediately diffused; however, by modeling the behavior you expect from your child, you can at least prevent it from escalating. Test out this strategy for proof. During normal conversation with your child, experiment by raising and lowering the volume of your voice. Your child will naturally mimic you without realizing it.

Another strategy that can be helpful in some instances for behavior modification is mirroring. By copying some of your child's body language, you can often deescalate the situation by sending an unspoken message that mommy or daddy still loves and accepts you exactly the way you are. I certainly do not mean to throw things, scream, or spit, if that is what she is exhibiting; however, subtly copying her hand placement, stance, or expression, can sometimes be helpful in diffusing the situation when coupled with a gentle, loving tone and eye contact.

TAMING THE SHREW
-HOW TO DIFFUSE A MELTDOWN-

As adults, when we see children become emotionally upset, our natural tendency is to immediately try to solve the problem. However, at the moment your child loses his mind, the capacity for logic and reasoning is nowhere to be found.

What do I need to know? From *The Whole Brain Child*, "...the left brain cares about the *letter of the law*...As you know, as kids get older they get really good at using this left-brain thinking: 'I didn't shove her! I pushed her.' The right brain, on the other hand, cares about the *spirit of the law*, the emotions and experiences of relationships. The left focuses on the text — the right is about the context." (Bryson & Siegel, 2011).

What can I do? As we have already discussed, step one is to model the behavior you expect. Physically get down to your child's level and speak to him using a quiet, gentle tone of voice. Step two is to begin helping your child out of the hysteria and back to a place of reason. Wonderfully put, Drs. Bryson and Siegel have coined the term "connect and redirect," which encourages parents to first connect with your child's emotional right brain, then redirect him to the logical, problem-solving left brain.

Young children need to know that they have been heard, and that their feelings are acknowledged before negotiation becomes possible. By simply making eye contact and saying, "I see you are upset", you let your little one know that his tears are recognized. It will likely take several tries and a great deal of patience; however, by using this connect and redirect approach, you will validate his feelings, encourage him to express himself and, once he calms down, be able to appropriately introduce logic, the possibility for negotiation, and direct him towards a resolution.

THE SKY IS FALLING
-RECOGNIZING A MELTDOWN IS COMING-

Young children are unpredictable and there are many times when poor, unsuspecting parents get absolutely no warning that a meltdown is coming. When this happens, modeling expected behavior and then connecting with what your little one is feeling so that you can then redirect, is the place to start. However, in those rare and coveted instances when you are actually graced with a little warning that critical mass is approaching, knowing how to stop it in its tracks can be a lifesaver.

What do I need to know? Keep your child talking and answering questions. This will keep him operating in the realm of logic and reason (Siegel and Bryson, 2011). In this realm, it is almost impossible to cross over into the irrational emotion-based behavior that accompanies a tantrum. On the contrary, if you become flustered and react by scolding or threatening punishment, the emotion of the moment will escalate because your child will follow your example.

What can I do? An example of successfully employing all of the techniques discussed thus far, is brought to us by my own step-son Jonathan (nickname "Jono"), now a grown man, who at the age of two-and-a-half, had an incident of nearly epic proportion over egg drop soup.

Our family had stepped out to our favorite Chinese restaurant for dinner. Knowing full well that Jono was never going to eat an entire bowl of soup, my husband suggested they share. Before he could finish speaking the words, the look on Jono's face changed and in an instant he was under the table. Recognizing that we were about 30 seconds from launch into hysteria, I joined Jono under the table and began to ask him questions:

 – "Jono, look at my eyes, what color are they?" (Engage. Use your child's name and get him to make eye contact.)

– "Jono, I see you are under the table. Are you upset about the soup?"(Remember the seven second rule, and wait for his answer.)

– "Do you want your own bowl of soup?" (Connect with what your child is feeling and honor his answer.)

– "Yes? That's great! Will you help me tell the waitress?" (Redirect your child by involving him in what comes next.)

Remembering in these moments to engage your child in external communication will help to quell the "internal talking" and emotional ramp-up that is going on in his mind that can easily devolve into a meltdown.

CROCODILE TEARS?
-KNOWING WHEN TO REACT-

When your child suddenly bursts into tears, it can be very trying. Seeing your child sad is very hard, and can leave you feeling frustrated and confused. It can be very challenging to toe the line between action and overreaction.

What do I need to know? Crying is not all that complicated. If your child commences closed-eyed-open-mouth bawling, with dry cheeks and just a lot of noise, then it is likely that you are the victim of a preschool power-play. We have already discussed how little ones learn to push your buttons very early on, by honing in on certain actions or "hot-button" words, and crying is by far one of the fastest and most effective producers of a reaction from mom or dad.

What can I do? Look for real tears. Tears are almost always a clear indicator of real physical pain or real emotional sadness, especially in very young children.

No matter how flabbergasted you feel in the moment, pause and really stop to look at your child. If you see tears, suspend opinion, put judgment aside and start asking her questions: "Does something hurt?"; "Did X make you feel sad?" However, if there are no tears to be found, then ignoring or redirecting her attention are likely your best options.

LYING AND HITTING AND WHINING, OH MY!
-TESTING LIMITS-

When my very tired, very hungry, three-and-a-half-year-old godson realized that he was *not* going to use my bathroom scissors to cut his own hair, and his response was to haul off and slap me across the face, my first thought was definitely *not,* "My goodness, look at this clear indicator of the cognitive development of a preschool-age child."

Young children learn by testing limits. As your little one grows up, expect that he is going to act-out. This is a completely normal way for children, especially preschoolers, to react to situations they dislike or do not have any control over (**Berman, 2010**). I am most frequently asked by parents about how to address lying, hitting, and whining which Karen Bannan, of *Parents Magazine*, has done a wonderful job of summarizing. Looking at each of these behaviors, keep in mind that successfully guiding your child toward the behavior you expect involves two key elements: firm limits and real consequences.

Lying – What do I need to know? Young children do not lie to be malicious. They do not yet understand that "not true" equals "wrong." Three and four-year-old children generally tell two kinds of lies: lies of self-preservation and lies of fantasy. A child will lie about smearing chocolate pudding on the dog to avoid the inevitable punishment. The same child will also tell all his friends at school that Spiderman came to his house for dinner last night because the line between fantasy and reality is still blurry at this young age.

What can I do? Point out the lie without sounding judgmental or angry. Often lying is simply wishful thinking, so acknowledge it. You might say, "I realize you wanted Daddy to *say* that you could have chocolate ice cream for dinner, but I know that he actually didn't, so you are going to have to eat your pasta first." Eventually your child will learn that telling tall tales is not going to work. Punishment is not the answer to lying at this age because your imaginative three-year-old might actually believe some of what he is saying. A frank discussion about the importance of telling the truth will make much more sense and will be far more effective.

Hitting – What do I need to know? The transition from being a toddler to becoming a preschooler is frustrating for children. Even though they now have a much greater expressive vocabulary, when something is really upsetting, preschoolers still cannot always spit out the words fast enough or with sufficient detail to get their point across. So, when your daughter does not want to share a toy but can't articulate her feelings before it is snatched away, she may resort to hitting.

What can I do? Let your child know that hitting is not okay. Again, keep your cool and teach her how to use words to fix the problem. It is empowering for children to learn how to negotiate. As a parent, you can create opportunities where negotiation is okay and you will accept the reached compromise. As we have already discussed, in the middle of a tantrum, negotiation will have to wait. Make eye contact and acknowledge her feelings first, then encourage your child to express the source of frustration: "I see that you are upset" (wait seven seconds); "Did you want to use the scissors to cut your hair?" (wait seven more seconds). "Tell me why." Be patient and ask as many times as necessary to get your child's answer. Using this approach, I actually learned that my godson had a curl that was poking him in the eye. We used the opportunity to talk about what a hair salon is, and the fact that there are people who are much better at cutting hair because it is their job. When we arrived at the salon, I was in the position to allow him to negotiate my giving up control and empower him to tell the hairdresser exactly what he wanted.

Whining – What do I need to know? Whining is an expression of discontent. Three and four-year-old children also very quickly figure out that whining is a very effective method for getting your attention, so it becomes the go-to voice when your little one feels upset or wants something (Hoffman, 2007).

What can I do? As irritating as whining can be to endure, it is important to once again, remain calm. Do not lash out. Your negative attention will only reinforce the behavior. Simply explain to your child that you cannot understand what he is saying. Explain that you would be happy to help with whatever the problem is; however, he will have to speak clearly in order for you to do so. If the whining continues, hold your ground and repeat the instruction. Ignoring the behavior will not work; it will only escalate since a whining child is usually a tired child. So breathe, keep your cool, and remember you have the upper hand – if your child really wants the thing he is whining for, surrender is inevitable.

TAKING "TIME-IN"
-APPROACHING DISCIPLINE POSITIVELY-

Some time ago, as a reasonable option to corporal or demeaning punishments, the "time-out" method became the buzzword for modern discipline. While originally the intent was a good one, it has basically turned into a newer version of "Go to your room!"– not exactly a highly effective form of progressive discipline. "This prevalent form of discipline makes a child experience a feeling of rejection and learn that love or inclusion will be withdrawn if he or she does not conform to the wishes of the adult" (Jacobs, 2015).

What do I need to know? Misbehaving is often a call for help with a problem or some needed encouragement, love, and understanding. Helping your child to verbalize her feelings often is enough to continue to problem solve. Time-out is relatively ineffective with very young children because the basic concept of taking time away from a situation to mull over one's actions or reactions, is far too abstract. In the same way that "I'm sorry," does not translate in the mind of a young child, "time-out," simply becomes either "the thing you have to do", or "the place you have to sit", when you are "bad", without any kind of real understanding.

What can I do? Spend "time-in" with your child. Approaching discipline from the point of view of inclusion and not exclusion, will have you both feeling more secure and in control. Time-in is all about taking proactive steps to prevent an issue from arising, rather than enacting punishment after the fact. Anticipate and prepare for challenging situations – it is far better to have a change of clothing, extra diapers, toys, bottle, and not need it, than to need it and not have it. Have appropriate expectations for your child's behavior based on her age and abilities. If your two-year-old has not napped, do not go out to a fancy restaurant. Be willing to adjust your plans accordingly. Take games, storybooks or quiet activities for waiting time in the doctor's office, car trips, restaurant-outings, or flights. Support your child by explaining the reasons for requests. Make clear, brief, and age-appropriate explanations: "You may not do X. It is not safe."

Intervene at the first moment you notice frustration developing. Just like noticing that the look on Jono's face changed in the Chinese restaurant, know your child's physical cues that indicate an ensuing meltdown, and either change the activity or just assist in making it easier to handle.

SEND IN THE REINFORCEMENTS
-UNDERSTANDING BEHAVIOR
MODIFICATION-

Reward (or reinforcement) and punishment are basic strategies that many parents use when disciplining their children. Often parents express to me that they try these strategies and find them to be unsuccessful. The problem usually boils down to the fact that these concepts can be a bit confusing, and often parents do not fully understand the difference between discipline and behavior modification, the different types of reinforcement and punishment, and their purpose.

What do I need to know? Reinforcement and punishment come in two forms – positive and negative. Do not think of these terms as "good" and "bad", but rather as "adding" or "subtracting." These strategies of reinforcement and punishment come from a theory called Operant Conditioning, developed by behaviorist B.F. Skinner, and their sole purpose to encourage or discourage a behavior.

Reinforcement and punishment are not discipline strategies that will teach your child empathy, compassion, accountability, or any level of higher thinking. They do one thing and only thing only – modify behavior.

What can I do? If you choose to implement one of these strategies to address behavior, know how to do so correctly. Reinforcement means you want the behavior to continue. Punishment means you want the behavior to disappear. Positive means you add something. Negative means you take something away. That is it. Below are some examples from real parents to help clarify:

Positive Reinforcement – "When Jacqueline ate all of her vegetables at dinner, we allowed her to have a chocolate chip cookie for dessert." Jacqueline's parents *added* the chocolate chip cookie because they wanted her vegetable-eating behavior to *continue*.

Positive Punishment – "When Peter wouldn't stop biting his fingernails, I applied that awful-tasting stuff from the pharmacy." Peter's mom *added* the bitter polish because she wanted his nail-biting behavior to *stop*.

Negative Reinforcement – "When Emil got all A's on his report card, I let him skip doing his chores for one week." Emil's mom *removed* his chores because she wanted his straight A's to *continue*.

Negative Punishment – "When Grace threw her toys all over the living room and refused to pick them up, I took away her iPad time for two days." Grace's dad *removed* her iPad time because he wanted her toy-throwing behavior to *stop*.

"IT'S TIME"
-SUCCESS IS 90% PREPARATION-

As a parent, you are the one who is responsible for planning, coordinating, and making appointments. In the day-to-day hustle of keeping your family's schedule, it is very easy to forget what your little one might be experiencing and feeling. Young children often feel at a loss of control in their lives because the grownups are in charge of making everything happen.

What do I need to know? We have already discussed how authentic choices give young children a sense of control and a feeling of empowerment. The same holds true for discussing your daily plan and giving your child a timeframe for exactly what is expected by you as the parent. Just like pick-up time from school, this can be another great opportunity to encourage conversation to offer some of those all-important authentic choices.

What can I do? In a nutshell, let your child know what is going on. Take a few minutes over breakfast to talk about the plan for the day: "After you finish lunch, we are going to the grocery store, and then it will be nap time. Later, Nana is coming over for dinner." In addition, prepare your child for what is coming and exactly what is expected: "When this cartoon ends, it will be time to get dressed." Take note that phrases such as "in five minutes" are ineffectual with very young children because they have no concept of actual time. However, they certainly can understand the idea of "now" and "later", or concrete examples of time such as "when this cartoon ends." Add to this by possibly including an authentic choice: "When this cartoon ends, it will be time to get dressed. Would you like to wear this blue shirt or this grey shirt?" Taking the time to include your little one in discussion of your daily itinerary, informing him of your exact expectations, asking for his opinion, and including some authentic choices, will send a clear message that your child's participation is important and valued, and will set you up for a successful day together.

MONSTERS IN THE CLOSET
-DEALING WITH FEAR-

Fear is a normal part of life for all of us, including young children. Fear most often arises when you try something new, experience something that you have never experienced before, or are confronted with something that is an unknown.

What do I need to know? Young children are exploring the world for the first time, so the potential for experiencing fear can happen on almost a daily basis. My dear friend Theresa, once shared a story with me about her niece's terrifying experience with "scary chicky," where a seemingly cute and quite innocuous stuffed Easter toy turned into trembling, lip-quivering, borderline-hysteria for poor two-year-old Veronica who could not be consoled until said chicky was properly scolded and flung clear across the living room.

Whether it is fear of the dark, fear of a TV show, fear of going to a new place, fear of a new person, or fear

of a stuffed chicky, your best approach as the parent is to communicate, be respectful, and show that you understand.

What can I do? First, avoid becoming frustrated. It can be heartbreaking to see your little one frightened and your natural reaction might be to quickly point out that "there is nothing to be afraid of"; however, the fear is very real for your child whether you see it as justified or not. Demonstrate respect. Never tell your child that she is "being silly." Not only will this not ease the fear, but now she will also feel ashamed and guilty for being frightened. Finally, empower your little one to address the fear. Talk to your child and ask what you can do together to help her feel better. For very young children, this can be an ideal time to offer choices to help the thought process along, such as bringing a known comfort item, or having mommy hold her hand.

ERR ON THE SIDE OF MANNERS
-SETTING CHILDREN UP FOR SUCCESS-

"To leave a better planet for our children, we must leave better children for our planet." (Unknown)

Effectively educating the children goes far beyond academics. Little ones must be taught the lessons that will help them to be successful beyond the classroom walls – self-confidence, independent thinking, and respect for oneself and for others. In our current social climate, manners can be easily forgotten. Children see examples of this almost daily, whether in the streets, on the train, or watching Saturday morning cartoons. To truly be successful in today's world, children still need to learn the societal rules and cultural references in their homes, classrooms, and greater environments.

What do I need to know? One of my favorite examples comes from a question I have been asked year after year, during admissions interviews: "Why do the children refer to the teachers as 'Ms.', or 'Mrs.', and not by their first names?" The answer is quite simply that in some social situations it might be acceptable to refer to an adult by their first name; however, this is certainly not true in all cases. Assuming it is acceptable to address a friend's mommy by her first name might open a child up to a negative experience when he finds out that in fact it is not okay.

What can I do? Err on the side of teaching your child to use formal manners first, such as greeting a friend's mommy as "Ms." or "Mrs." So-and-so. This will either be the correct choice from the get-go, or will open the door to be invited by the adult to use her first name, giving your child a successful and positive social experience. There are many other examples such as learning to use a tissue, what to do when meeting a new person, or how to properly wait one's turn. In all of these, employing grace and courtesy sets children up to be successful in the given social situation, which in turn fosters confidence, positive self-esteem, and a sense of accomplishment. Now, wouldn't we all like to feel that way?

ABOUT THE AUTHOR

Bridie Gauthier is the Head of School of the Montessori School of Manhattan. Bridie co-founded MSM in 2002. In 2011, she launched a charitable outreach project, raising the capital which built a preschool for two and three-year-old children in the impoverished Batey Lecheria, Dominican Republic.

Born and raised in Ontario, Canada, Bridie has been an educator of young children for 30 years. She left Canada for the bright lights of New York City in 1995, where she met and married her husband Joe. Bridie shares her time running MSM, travelling to the Dominican Republic, to conduct faculty training seminars and to work hands-on with the children of the Batey, and spending time with the full-time joy in her life, her godson Kai.

Practical life for Parents is a collection of tips, hints, and advice that Bridie has offered to real parents, living real lives, raising real kids.

REFERENCES

Bannan, Karen. "Preschoolers Behaving Badly". *Parents.com*.
October, 2010 issue of *Parents Magazine*.
>   <http://www.parents.com/toddlers-
>   preschoolers/development/behavioral/preschoolers-
>   behaving-badly>

Berman, Jenn. *SuperBaby: 12 Ways to Give Your Child a Head Start
in the First 3 Years*. New York: Sterling, 2010. Print.

Crosser, Sandra. "Would You Like an Apple or a Banana? Why
Offering Toddlers Choices Is Important." *Earlychildhood NEWS*.
>   <http://www.earlychildhoodnews.com/earlychildhood/ar
>   ticle_view.aspx?ArticleID=691>

Gavigan, Julian. "Be careful what you say! Babies learn meaning
of words months earlier than first thought." *Daily Mail*.
February, 2012.
>   <http://www.dailymail.co.uk/health/article-
>   2100540/Infants-start-understanding-meaning-words-
>   months-earlier-thought.html#ixzz3pxo92Ore>

Hamilton, John. "Scientists Say Child's Play Helps Build A
Better Brain." *NPREd*. August, 2014.
>   <http://www.npr.org/sections/ed/2014/08/06/3363612
>   77/scientists-say-childs-play-helps-build-a-better-brain>

Hoffman, Norman. *Bad Children Can Happen to Good Parents*.
Florida: VG Press, 2007. Print.

Montessori Unlimited. "The Fine Art of Sharing". *Articles for
Parents*. 2015.
>   <http://www.montessori.com/parent-resource-
>   center/parenting-articles/the-fine-art-of-sharing>

Siegel, Daniel and Payne-Bryson, Tina. *The Whole Brain Child*.
New York: Bantam, 2012. Print.

INDEX

www.ingramcontent.com/pod-product-compliance
Lightning Source LLC
Chambersburg PA
CBHW071234280526
45787CB00002B/929